Shake, Sizzle, and Stir

BLACK RABBIT BOOKS

Black Rabbit Books
P.O. Box 227
Mankato, MN 56001
www.blackrabbitbooks.com

Library edition published in 2026 by Black Rabbit Books.
This library-bound edition is reprinted by arrangement with Rebel Girls, Inc.

Text by Calliope Glass | Illustrations by Laura Borio
Art direction by Giulia Flamini | Cover design by Kristen Brittain

Cataloging-in-Publication Data is available at the Library of Congress.
ISBN 978-1-64582-576-0

Printed in China

Shake, Sizzle, and Stir

Tales of Extraordinary Women

Written by Calliope Glass
Illustrated by Laura Borio

Roll, press, and squish pastry dough

like
Julia!

Chop,
dice,
and
mince
veggies

like
Leah!

Shake, sizzle, and stir spices

like
Asma!

Plant, pull, and pick ingredients

like
Alice!

Cook, record, and celebrate your love of food

like
Maangchi!

Bake, decorate,
and taste
brilliant
cakes

like
Nadiya!

Scribble, jot, and write recipes

like
Edna!

Taste,
create,
and share
new dishes

like
Padma!

Stir in spices!
Plant a garden!
Taste something
new!

These women made food that brought people together. One day, you can too.

JULIA CHILD

Born on August 15, 1912, Julia Child was an American chef, author, and television personality who introduced French cuisine to American households. Her cookbook *Mastering the Art of French Cooking* and her popular TV show, *The French Chef*, made her a beloved culinary icon. Julia's deep love of cooking and her adventurous spirit encouraged many people to experiment in the kitchen.

LEAH CHASE

Leah Chase was born in 1923 in Louisiana. She and her family grew up eating fresh fruits and vegetables from her dad's farm. In high school, Leah met her husband, and together they started running his family's restaurant. It became the only fine dining restaurant for Black folks in Louisiana. Known as the Queen of Creole Cuisine, Leah served up delicious dishes to her community seven days a week.

ASMA KHAN

Asma Khan, born in July 1969, is an Indian-born British chef and restaurateur who has made it her mission to empower and employ women from South Asian backgrounds. She founded Darjeeling Express, a restaurant that serves authentic Indian cuisine and is staffed by an all-female team. Asma's commitment to social justice and her delicious, traditional dishes show the world how food can create opportunities and bring people together.

ALICE WATERS

Born on April 28, 1944, Alice Waters is an American chef, restaurateur, and food activist who champions the farm-to-table movement. Her influential restaurant, Chez Panisse, focuses on locally sourced, organic ingredients. Alice's dedication to sustainability and environmental responsibility has transformed the way many people think about food and its connection to the earth.

NADIYA HUSSAIN

Nadiya Hussain was born in England in 1984. Nadiya's dad was a chef, but she didn't take up baking until she was in her 20s. Nadiya started watching a baking show called *The Great British Bake Off.* With her family's encouragement, she entered the competition. Nadiya's incredible creations wowed the judges, and she was crowned the winner! Since then, Nadiya has written books and become the host of her own cooking shows.

MAANGCHI

Maangchi, born on April 12, 1957, is a South Korean chef, YouTube personality, and cookbook author known for her vibrant and accessible approach to Korean cooking. With her cheerful demeanor and easy-to-follow recipes, Maangchi has introduced millions of viewers to the flavors of Korean cuisine. Her passion for sharing her culinary heritage and her ability to connect with people through food have made her an inspiration for home cooks and food lovers alike.

EDNA LEWIS

Edna Lewis, born on April 13, 1916, was a chef and food writer who celebrated the flavors of Southern cuisine. Her cookbooks, such as *The Taste of Country Cooking*, preserve the culinary heritage of the American South and highlight the importance of farm-fresh, seasonal ingredients. Edna's warm storytelling and mouthwatering recipes make her a role model for many young chefs.

PADMA LAKSHMI

Born in India in 1970, Padma Lakshmi is a bestselling author, food expert, and television host. For her television shows, she has traveled all over the world trying new flavors and cuisines. She has also shared her own recipes in several cookbooks. Padma's work spotlights how enriching it is to go on adventures and try new things.

FLOUR